WOMEN IN THE ARTS

WOMEN IN Film

BY NADINE PINEDE, PHD

CONTENT CONSULTANT
Suzanne Leonard, PhD
Associate Professor
Simmons College

Cover image: Melissa McCarthy starred in the 2016 film *Ghostbusters*.

Core Library
An Imprint of Abdo Publishing
abdopublishing.com

abdopublishing.com

Published by Abdo Publishing, a division of ABDO, PO Box 398166, Minneapolis, Minnesota 55439.

Printed in the United States of America, North Mankato, Minnesota
042018
092018

Cover Photo: Gregg DeGuire/WireImage/Getty Images
Interior Photos: Gregg DeGuire/WireImage/Getty Images, 1; Jordan Strauss/Invision/AP Images, 4–5; Walt Disney Studios Motion Pictures/Photofest, 7, 19; Paramount Pictures/Photofest, 8–9; Richard Shotwell/Invision/AP Images, 11, 24–25; John Shearer/Invision/AP Images, 14–15; Joel Ryan/Invision/AP Images, 17; Warner Bros/Photofest, 20, 45; Red Line Editorial, 21, 39; Sthanlee B. Mirador/Sipa/AP Images, 26; Matt Sayles/AP Images, 30; Twentieth Century Fox Film Corporation/ Photofest, 32–33, 43; Matt Sayles/Invision/AP Images, 35, 40; Eric Charbonneau/Invision/Netflix/ AP Images, 37

Editor: Marie Pearson
Imprint Designer: Maggie Villaume
Series Design Direction: Claire Vanden Branden

Library of Congress Control Number: 2017962834

Publisher's Cataloging-in-Publication Data

Names: Pinede, Nadine, author.
Title: Women in film / by Nadine Pinede.
Description: Minneapolis, Minnesota : Abdo Publishing, 2019. | Series: Women in the arts | Includes online resources and index.
Identifiers: ISBN 9781532114755 (lib.bdg.) | ISBN 9781532154584 (ebook)
Subjects: LCSH: Female actors--Juvenile literature. | Women motion picture producers and directors--United States--Juvenile literature. | Women in the performing arts--Juvenile literature.
Classification: DDC 791.43--dc23

CONTENTS

CHAPTER ONE

Motivational Movies

Television audiences around the world held their breath. It was the end of a long night. It was time to announce the 2015 Academy Award for Best Motion Picture. The awards, also known as the Oscars, highlight the best work in the movie industry. Being nominated for an Oscar is a big deal.

Ava DuVernay sat with other excited nominees in the glitzy Hollywood theater. She had directed a film about Dr. Martin Luther King Jr. and the civil rights movement. *Selma* had received glowing reviews. It was nominated for Best Motion Picture.

Director Ava DuVernay's film *Selma* was nominated for Best Motion Picture at the 2015 Oscars.

DuVernay was the first black woman to direct a Best Motion Picture nominee.

DuVernay didn't expect to hear her name called—and it wasn't. But she was still a winner. Her film was successful in other ways.

DuVernay did not go to film school. Her first job in the movie business was promoting other films. What she learned helped her make her own movies. She spent $50,000 of her own money to create her first film, *I Will Follow*.

A $100 Million Movie

DuVernay directed *A Wrinkle in Time* (2018), a film based on Madeleine L'Engle's fantasy novel. The project made her the first black woman to direct a live-action movie with a $100 million budget. She was only the third woman to do so. The star-filled cast includes Reese Witherspoon, Oprah Winfrey, and Mindy Kaling. Storm Reid plays the lead character, Meg Murry. Meg, an ordinary high school student, must rescue her father from prison on another planet. DuVernay was excited about the opportunity to create a film with a minority heroine.

DuVernay, *left*, directed the 2018 film *A Wrinkle in Time*, which features Storm Reid as main character Meg Murry.

Released in 2010, the film tells the story of a young woman who takes care of her sick aunt. DuVernay used the profits to make another movie.

***Selma* was nominated for a Best Motion Picture Oscar.**

Today, DuVernay is an influential film director. She makes a point of hiring women and members of racial minorities to work on her films. She has more than 1.8 million followers on Twitter. She has received many awards. She even has a Barbie doll based on her.

SELMA

DuVernay's film *Selma* takes place in Alabama in 1965. At the time, black people and white people were kept separate in schools, stores, and restaurants. Many places didn't allow black people to vote. Some people

#OscarsSoWhite

The 2015 Oscars caused a commotion. No minority actors were nominated in the acting categories. The same thing had happened in 2014. Other films about African Americans were overlooked as well.

People thought that the Oscars should reflect the diversity of modern society. The social media movement #OscarsSoWhite was born. In response, the Academy made some changes. The group plans to double its number of women and minority members by 2022. Current members must stay active in the industry to vote on the Oscars.

tried to peacefully protest. It didn't always end well. During one protest in March 1965, police officers hurt more than 50 people.

Selma tells the story of when Dr. Martin Luther King Jr. came to Selma, Alabama, to lead a protest. He teamed up with others for a 50-mile (80 km) march to support racial equality. The march helped convince President Johnson to pass the Voting Rights Act of 1965. The law made it illegal to try to prevent black Americans from voting.

DuVernay, *left*, and songwriter Common won several Emmy Awards for the documentary *13th*.

A WAY TO DO BETTER

When DuVernay was a little girl, her aunt Denise often took her to the movies. They would talk about problems in the world. Today, DuVernay is not afraid to tackle difficult subjects. She created the documentary *13th*.

It explores how black people are treated unfairly by the law. The film argues that the courts punish black people more harshly than white people. DuVernay argues that prison is a new form of slavery.

DuVernay wants to inspire people. She was described by *Time* magazine as a woman who is changing the world. Her films, including *Selma*, are known for their raw emotional power. Some people watch movies to escape the world. DuVernay makes movies to change the world.

STRAIGHT TO THE SOURCE

In *Selma*, DuVernay focused on sound design to make an impact:

The sound design for that bridge sequence is something I'm very proud of. . . . Whenever there's any kind of violence to the body, sound becomes critical.

We spent a lot of time . . . trying to perfect which sound I wanted to choose for when a baton hit the body. And there were different levels of that . . . you felt it in your heart when you heard it. Because I think what we were trying to do with this whole film is to just elevate it from a page in your history book and really just get it into your body—into your DNA.

Source: Terri Gross. "The Sounds, Space and Spirit of '*Selma*': A Director's Take." *Movie Interviews*. NPR, January 8, 2015. Web. Accessed October 27, 2017.

Changing Minds

This text passage discusses how and why DuVernay focused on sound in a violent scene. Do you think that sounds are the best way to convey the emotion of a scene? Imagine your best friend has a different opinion. Write a short essay trying to change your friend's mind. Make sure you include facts and details that support your position.

CHAPTER TWO

In the Spotlight

Imagine going from being a drama school student to winning an Oscar in less than a year. That was Lupita Nyong'o's path to stardom. Her first feature film was *12 Years a Slave*. The movie tells the true story of a free black man sold into slavery. Nyong'o played an enslaved person who is mistreated by her slaveholder. She won an Oscar for Best Actress in a Supporting Role.

Nyong'o was born in Mexico City, Mexico, and she was raised in Kenya. She was the first Mexican-born and first Kenyan actress to win an Oscar. Nyong'o is also a fashion icon. She is

In 2014, Lupita Nyong'o won Best Actress in a Supporting Role for the film *12 Years a Slave*.

often mentioned on best-dressed lists. *People* magazine even named her the "most beautiful person in the world."

But Nyong'o says that she wants to be known for her acting, not her physical appearance. She played Maz Kanata in *Star Wars: The Force Awakens*. The short, big-eyed alien was created using motion capture. This technology uses human movements to make a computer-generated character. Nyong'o also played the spy and action hero Nakia in *Black Panther*.

Melissa McCarthy: Redefining Image

Many movies and television shows hire only slender, tall women for the main roles. But McCarthy hasn't let her height or weight stop her from becoming a successful actress. She's starred in many comedies, including the 2011 film *Bridesmaids*. The highly-praised comedy was written by Kristen Wiig, who also had the leading role. McCarthy's comical performance in the film was widely loved. She earned a nomination from the Academy Awards for Best Supporting Actress.

Auli'i Cravalho voiced the title character in the 2016 film *Moana*.

Nyong'o wrote about experiencing harassment as a young actress. Her story was one of many that inspired the #MeToo March on November 12, 2017. The march started in Hollywood, California. Thousands of people participated. Celebrities such as Oprah Winfrey, Reese Witherspoon, and Natalie Portman joined the cause too.

MAJOR TALENT

Most actresses start out with small roles and work their way up. It is rare that a young actress starts her career with a major role. Auli'i Cravalho was only 14 years old when she auditioned to become the voice of Moana. She was the very last girl to audition. She didn't think she was good enough. Luckily, a talent agent disagreed. Auli'i accepted the role of Moana.

Auli'i is proud of her Native Hawaiian culture and the Polynesian traditions shown in the film. *Moana* shows how Polynesians used the stars to explore the seas long before Europeans did. Auli'i continues to accept major roles. She stars in the show *Rise*, about a high school drama club. It premiered in March 2018.

WOMEN AT THE BOX OFFICE

Male actors usually make more money than female actors do. Women's contributions are often undervalued and underappreciated. Men and women also tend to star in different types of movies. Action and superhero movies usually make a lot of money at the box office. Action movies often have many more male characters than female characters.

Women in the industry say there is a solution. Companies should create more films with women at the center. Several 2017 blockbusters had female lead

Daisy Ridley, who plays Rey, is one of the stars of the blockbuster hit *Star Wars: The Last Jedi*.

characters. *Star Wars: The Last Jedi* made the most money of any 2017 movie. One of the main characters is Rey. She is training to become a Jedi warrior.

Wonder Woman was another successful movie. It tells the story of Diana, a superhero known as Wonder Woman. It is set during World War I (1914–1918). There are many female characters. It even had a female director, Patty Jenkins. Many people were excited to see a female superhero.

Actress Gal Gadot, *left*, and director Patty Jenkins discuss a scene in the 2017 film *Wonder Woman*.

Film actresses are often in the spotlight, but they are not always treated respectfully. Many actresses have found it difficult to change how women are treated in the film industry.

SPEAKING UP

Many of today's top actresses use their influence to speak up for causes. Three-time Oscar winner Meryl Streep is known as one of the best actresses in the world. She has a long career in major roles. But she was worried that her career would be over after she turned 40 in 1989. Not many roles are created for women her age.

WOMEN'S SPEAKING ROLES IN FILMS

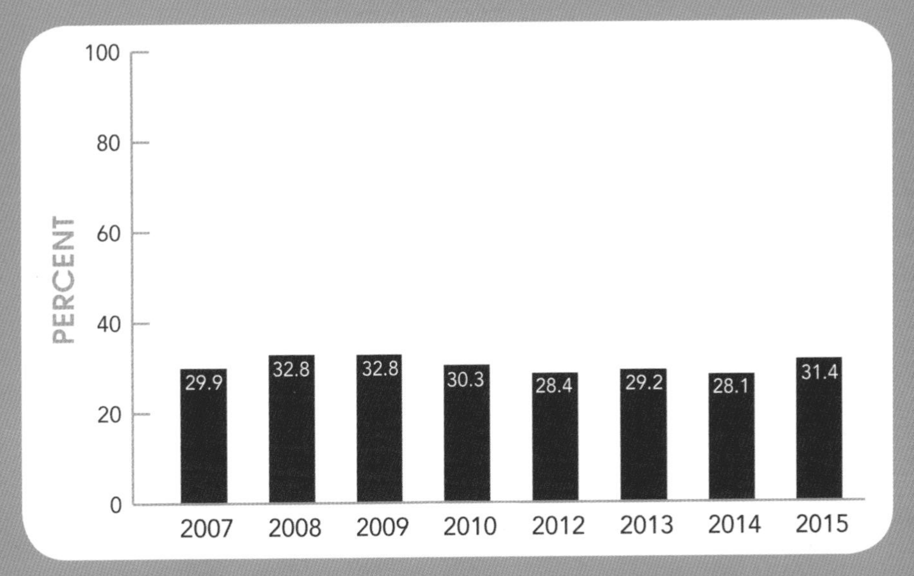

Roughly one-third of speaking characters in films released from 2007 to 2015 are women. How many women were in the last movie you saw? How many of them had a speaking part? Why do you think there are fewer women than men with speaking roles? (2011 data unavailable.)

In 2014, Streep played the witch in *Into the Woods.* She had turned down offers to play a witch when she was younger. She said such roles were given to women when Hollywood considered them old, even if they weren't. In 2014, she felt old enough for the part.

Older women are nearly invisible onscreen, even though their numbers in the United States are growing.

Many actresses who play mothers are only a few years older than the actors who play their children. Among actors and actresses older than 40, men received 80 percent of the leading roles from 1920 to 2011. Streep wants film roles for older women to be as interesting as they are for men.

Miss Representation

Hollywood has a long history of featuring women as simply victims or villains. Many films have defined female characters only by their appearances. Even today, many female characters don't play an active or important part in the story. Minority women, LGBT women, and women with disabilities are rarely seen in movies. The documentary *Miss Representation* tells how girls are affected by watching simplistic or sexualized depictions of women in movies, television, and commercials. It says that girls should be valued for their leadership abilities, not only their looks.

STRAIGHT TO THE SOURCE

After winning her Oscar, Nyong'o acted in the dramatic play *Eclipsed*. It was the first Broadway show to have an all-black and all-female cast and creative team. Nyong'o spoke about her experiences with the play:

> *You become a part of a larger conversation but you cannot live your life from that vantage point. You just have to live your life day by day, opportunity by opportunity, and make the most of it. The way the world sees success doesn't necessarily have to be the way you see success. So for me, I find winning the Academy Award was a major success and I am so grateful for it. But so was doing the play on Broadway, which for me was something huge that I was able to do. And it may not live in the public eye in the same way but for me, I feel like I've grown and gone to the next step.*

Source: Susan Wloszczyna. "The Next Step: Lupita Nyong'o on 'Queen of Katwe.'" *RogerEbert.com*. RogerEbert.com, September 21, 2016. Web. Accessed November 15, 2017.

What's the Big Idea?

Read this passage closely. What is the connection Nyong'o is making between the way she defines success and the way others might define it? What does she believe about her Broadway role, according to this excerpt?

CHAPTER
THREE

Lights, Camera, Action!

A film director works behind the camera. She makes important choices about how the film will look. She also helps decide who will play each part and how the film will sound. But it takes a whole team to make the director's vision a reality. Female directors work hard to increase their numbers. They tell stories that change how we see the world and each other.

Director Mira Nair's films are alive with color and music. Her family is from India. Her films include *Mississippi Masala, Monsoon Wedding*, and *Queen of Katwe*. They feature

Mira Nair directed *Queen of Katwe*.

Madina Nalwanga grew up in Uganda. She had never been in a film until she starred as Phiona Mutesi in *Queen of Katwe*.

girls and women who struggle to overcome real-life problems. Nair shoots her films on location with local actors.

In *Queen of Katwe*, Nair tells the true story of Phiona Mutesi. Mutesi came from a poor neighborhood in Uganda. Her father died when she was three years old. She was brought up by her mother. When Mutesi was eight or nine, she followed her brother to a club where he was playing chess. She walked 3.7 miles (6 km) every day to play chess.

When she was 13, she was part of the Ugandan chess team at an international African tournament. The team won. Mutesi's mother is played by Lupita Nyong'o. Nair wanted to show parts of African life that she did not see in Hollywood movies. She wanted

From Celebrity Daughter to Best Director

Sofia Coppola was first famous for being the daughter of director Francis Ford Coppola. Today, she is celebrated as a director in her own right. She made a movie called *Marie Antoinette*. The movie shows how the famous queen was not in control of her own life. In 2017, Coppola won the Best Director prize at the Cannes Film Festival in France for her film *The Beguiled*. The film tells the story of women at a Southern boarding school who care for a wounded soldier during the Civil War (1861–1865). Coppola was only the second woman in 70 years to win this prestigious prize.

to show that it takes family and community to help people reach their potential.

Stories to Tell

New Zealand's Jane Campion grew up shy and awkward. She never thought she would become a director. But she knew that movies made her feel connected to the world. She went to art school to study writing. No one was making films about the stories she wanted to tell, so she decided to make them herself. Her films, such as *The Piano* and *Angel at My Table*, as well as her television series *Top of the Lake*, are about complicated girls and women whom society considers outsiders. Her work has won international awards.

WOMEN BEHIND THE CAMERA

Directors used to be mainly men. But there have been important female directors throughout the years. Ida Lupino was an actress. She directed and produced films in the 1950s. Her films dealt with controversial issues.

Women have directed various films throughout history. But they didn't always get the awards they deserved. The Oscars started in 1929. Actresses have received awards since the beginning. But women were overlooked in other categories. No woman won the Oscar for Best Director until 2010, when Kathryn Bigelow won for *The Hurt Locker*, a drama about the Iraq War (2003–2011).

Today, more and more women are taking charge of films. But in the top 250 money-making films of 2016, women made up only 7 percent of film directors. The bigger a film's budget, the less likely a woman is to direct. Female directors are more common in independent films and documentaries.

TELLING UNTOLD STORIES

Documentaries are films that show real life and events. They help viewers see what it's like to walk in other people's shoes. Julie Cohen is a producer and director of documentary films. Cohen began her career on public television.

In *I Live to Sing*, Cohen follows three young black South African opera singers. They are from poor neighborhoods. Cohen asks them about apartheid, a system of racial segregation and discrimination. The film shows how art can help change lives.

Further Evidence

Chapter Three discusses female directors. Identify one of the chapter's main points. What evidence does the author provide to support her main point? Read the article at the website below. Does information on the website support the main point you identified? Or does it present new evidence?

Men Directed Three Times as Many Festival Films as Women in 2016

abdocorelibrary.com/women-in-film

Kathryn Bigelow received Oscars for Best Director and Best Picture for her film *The Hurt Locker*.

CHAPTER FOUR

Movies could never be made without people who work behind the scenes. Besides actors and a director, a movie crew includes writers, producers, film editors, camera operators, costume designers, makeup and hair stylists, publicists, and cinematographers. Each person plays a very important part in the success of a movie.

WHAT PRODUCERS DO

Oprah Winfrey works to create a more inclusive environment for women and minorities in film.

Starring as Katherine Johnson, Taraji P. Henson was the face of *Hidden Figures*. But it took many people behind the scenes to make the movie.

She was a producer on *Selma*. What does a producer do? The answer is, a little bit of everything! There is not a set career path for becoming a producer. Producers may work with screenwriters to develop a movie idea. They may hire directors and keep the film on budget and on schedule. After the film has been shot and edited, they may help get publicity for it.

Donna Gigliotti produced *Hidden Figures.* The movie tells how three black women helped put the first American

Beyond Hollywood

Hollywood has been the center of American filmmaking for decades. But online producers have created new business models for making and distributing films. Companies such as Amazon, Hulu, and Netflix are creating original content that can be watched on televisions, phones, or computers. Traditional movies rate their success by the number of tickets sold or the amount of money made. But online companies sell their shows as part of a package. This approach can support content that might not be made by regular studios. Women sometimes benefit from this approach.

Katherine Johnson, *seated*, is one of the real-life people portrayed in the Oscar-nominated film *Hidden Figures*.

astronauts into space. The film was nominated for a Best Picture Oscar in 2017. *Hidden Figures* had the most ticket sales of any Oscar-nominated film that year.

Lisa Nishimura is the daughter of Japanese immigrants. She is the vice president of original documentaries and comedies at Netflix. At Netflix, Nishimura worked with Ava DuVernay on the documentary *13th*. She has provided support to many films that feature women's voices and stories.

BEHIND THE CAMERA

Many important jobs performed by a film crew remain hidden to moviegoers. Women are still uncommon in film crews. Numbers aren't rising quickly. Some companies conduct surveys to find out how many women have these jobs. Women filled only 17 percent of the important behind-the-scenes jobs in 2016. The jobs surveyed included directors, writers, producers, executive producers, editors, and cinematographers. But despite their small numbers, women are working to make a difference.

Lisa Nishimura has led several Oscar-nominated projects.

Hidden No More

The book *Hidden Figures* describes the black female mathematicians who helped send the first American astronauts into space. The women had to work hard to break down barriers. Because it shows the vast influence of these unlikely heroines, the movie inspires kids to learn science. One screening had 10,000 girls attend. The cast and crew have been part of many panels about science and engineering jobs.

Screenwriters create scripts or adapt them from books. Screenwriter Allison Schroeder adapted *Hidden Figures.* It was a nonfiction book of the same name. She was nominated for an Oscar for that screenplay. Cinematographers are in charge of the lights and cameras that give the film its own special look. The Australian cinematographer Mandy Walker also worked on *Hidden Figures.*

Film editors help make sure the film makes sense. Joi McMillon was the first black woman nominated for an Oscar in this category. She was the film editor on

WHERE ARE THE WOMEN?

A study of 1,365 film creators between 2007 and 2015 found very few women. Women and girls make up more than half of the population in the United States. But very few directors, producers, and other crew members are women. What do you think are some reasons for this?

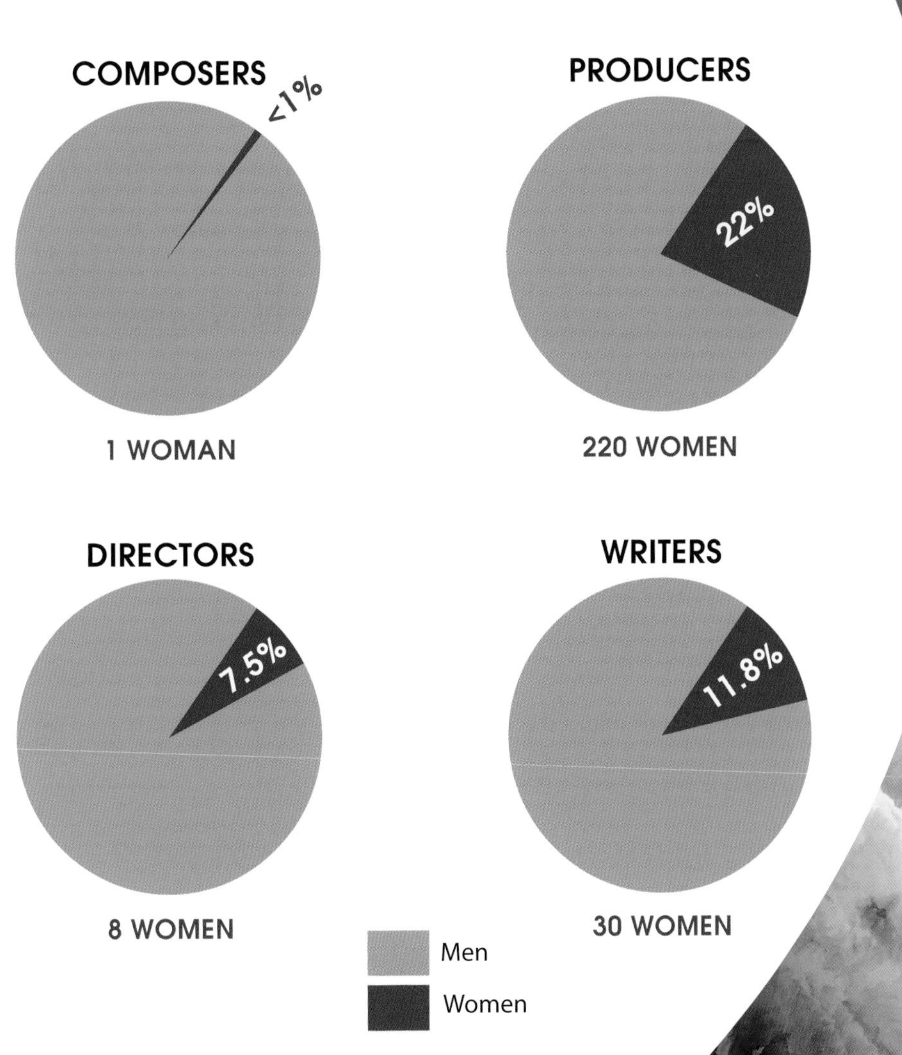

Film editor Joi McMillon, *left*, and actress Janelle Monáe celebrate the Best Picture win for *Moonlight*.

Moonlight, a coming-of-age story about a gay man. It had an all-black cast. In 2017, *Moonlight* became the first LGBT film to win the Best Picture Oscar.

Composers write music for films. Mica Levi composed the music for *Jackie*. The film tells the story of Jackie Kennedy, the wife of President John F. Kennedy. Levi was nominated for an Oscar for Best Original Score in 2017. She was the first woman nominated in more than a decade.

Thanks to new mobile and digital technologies, it is easier than ever to make films. Women's voices in film matter. Film can shape how we see ourselves and the world. Through the power of images, words, and sounds, film touches hearts and minds. Movies connect us to the world and each other.

Explore Online

Rachel Morrison became the first woman nominated for a cinematography Oscar with her 2017 film *Mudbound*. *Mudbound* tells the story of two poor Mississippi families in the late 1940s. Morrison writes about her career at the website below. What does Morrison say about the struggles of being a woman in the industry? How is it the same as what is mentioned in this chapter? How is it different?

A Cinematographer on Her Oscar History-Making Moment

abdocorelibrary.com/women-in-film

NOTABLE WORKS

Hidden Figures

Hidden Figures tells the story of the African American women who worked for NASA in the 1960s. The film follows three mathematicians as they work to send the first American astronaut into orbit. They face daily humiliations. These include segregated bathrooms, offices, and even coffeepots. Their intellect is constantly underestimated. Even so, the women work hard to overcome the racism and sexism of their time, and they triumph.

Selma

Ava DuVernay's film about Dr. Martin Luther King Jr. received glowing reviews and many awards. Dr. King is portrayed in the context of the community, his family, and the other brave people who risked their lives to fight racial discrimination. The film also shows the importance of girls and women in the civil rights movement.

Wonder Woman

Wonder Woman is a superhero film based on the DC Comics character Wonder Woman, who is Amazon warrior goddess Diana. Along with the female lead (Gal Gadot), the film had a female director (Patty Jenkins) and many other women in acting roles and working behind the scenes.

Queen of Katwe

Mira Nair lives in Kampala, the capital city of Uganda. She shot her film in the nearby slum of Katwe. This film is the coming-of-age story of Phiona Mutesi. She becomes a chess master. The film illustrates how her mother, her coach, and her community helped her achieve success.

STOP AND THINK

Tell the Tale

Chapter Three of this book explores the experiences of a documentary filmmaker. Imagine you are making a documentary film of your own. Write about the subject you would choose and why it is important to you. How will you find the people to film for your documentary, and how will you interact with them?

Another View

This book talks about women in several kinds of roles in the film industry. As you know, every source is different. Ask an adult to help you find another source about women in film and the challenges they face. Write a short essay comparing and contrasting the new source's point of view with that of this book's author. What is the point of view of each author? How are they similar and why? How are they different and why?

Why Do I Care?

You may never join the film industry. But that doesn't mean that women in film aren't changing life for everyone. Think about films that have had an impact on you, and why. How does film affect your life? How do the images of women in film affect how you see yourself? How would your life be different without movies?

You Are There

This book discusses several directors' films. Imagine that you are on a movie set to direct a film. Write 150 words about what you would do to make sure that the film shoot goes well. Where would you shoot your film? What directions would you give your actors and actresses? How would you describe shooting this film to your friends?

GLOSSARY

adapt
taking a book and making it into a movie or TV show

cinematographer
also called the director of photography, in charge of cameras and lighting

diversity
including different racial groups

documentary
a film or television series about real people and events

harassment
unwanted and repeated negative attention

independent films
movies not made by Hollywood studios, usually with less money

LGBT
LGBT stands for lesbian, gay, bisexual, and transgender

producer
someone responsible for making sure a movie gets made

score
the music composed for a movie

ONLINE RESOURCES

To learn more about women in film, visit our free resource websites below.

Visit **abdocorelibrary.com** for free Common Core resources for teachers and students, including vetted activities, multimedia, and booklinks, for deeper subject comprehension.

Visit **abdobooklinks.com** for free additional online weblinks for further learning. These links are routinely monitored and updated to provide the most current information available.

LEARN MORE

Blofield, Robert. *How to Make a Movie in 10 Easy Lessons: Learn How to Write, Direct, and Edit Your Own Film without a Hollywood Budget*. London, England: Walter Foster Jr., 2015.

INDEX

About the Author

Nadine Pinede, PhD, is the author of *An Invisible Geography*. She is also a contributing writer to *American Decade, Literary Newsmakers, Encyclopedia of African American Culture, Haiti Noir,* and *Becoming: What Makes a Woman*. Dr. Pinede edited "*True Colors:*" *Identity, Labeling & Global Colorism*.